Ellishia Allen, Killer: An anthology of True Crime

Pete Dove

Published by Trellis Publishing, 2021.

While every precaution has been taken in the preparation of this book, the publisher assumes no responsibility for errors or omissions, or for damages resulting from the use of the information contained herein.

ELLISHIA ALLEN, KILLER: AN ANTHOLOGY OF TRUE CRIME

First edition. July 8, 2021.

ISBN: 979-8215006474

Written by Pete Dove.

ELLISHIA ALLEN, KILLER

PETE DOVE

SARA ALDRETE AND THE SERIAL KILLERS OF DEVIL'S RANCH

2

EARLY LIFE

Sara Aldrete was born on September 6, 1964 in Matamoros, Tamaulipas, Mexico. As a teen, Sara was allowed to cross the border and attend Porter High School in Brownsville, Texas while her father supported the family working as an electrician. Teachers were fond of Sara as she was a well-behaved student who excelled academically. Her guidance counselor advised her to attend college immediately after graduation but Sara opted to marry instead. At the age of nineteen, she tied the knot with thirty-year old Miguel Zacharias on Halloween Day in 1983. The union did not last last, however, as they were separated and divorced within five months.

Two years later, Sara gained legal status as an American citizen. She enrolled at Texas Southmost College, a two-year school in Brownsville. She had been admitted on a work study program that minimized some of the tuition costs as she worked as both an aerobics teacher and assistant secretary in the school's athletic department.

Sara started classes in January of 1986 as a physical education major. At 6-feet-1 and with model good looks, she was a striking figure around campus.She became one of thirty-three students selected from over a 6,500 member student body to be included in the school's Who's Who directory for 1988. An active student on the campus, she organized a Booster club for the school's soccer squad as well as playing for the girl's volleyball team.

After the dissolution of her marriage, however, she had to move back home with her parents in Matamoros. They had constructed a patio/stairwell outside her second floor room so she could have some semblance of privacy. Sara came home on weekends and during the school breaks, hoping to transfer to a four-year program wherein she could receive a teaching certificate.

Her height and lithe physique caught the eye of many men, in particular Gilberto Sosa, a drug dealer who had ties with the powerful Hernandez family. She began dating Sosa while nurturing an interest in the religion of *Santería*. She learned about the religion's rituals and history during an anthropology class, immediately becoming obsessed. Ironically, this interest would coincide with meeting the man who would take her on a trip into darkness that she would never escape from.

"She would cross that border to Mexico," Lt George Gavito said. "And she would become somebody else."

GODFATHER AND GODMOTHER

Sara was driving through Matamoros on July 30th, 1987 when she nearly got into a car accident with a young man driving a luxury Mercedes-Benz. The young man got out of the car acting apolegetic. Sara was immediately taken by his good looks and well-spoken nature. His introduced himself as Adolfo Constanzo. They exchanged information and Adolfo expressed excitement when he learned that Sara shared the same birthday as his mother.

What Sara didn't know was that the near miss on the Matamoros street was carefully choreographed. Adolfo had been stalking Sara's boyfriend, Gilberto, assessing how much power he had in the drug dealing Hernandez organization.

Adolfo quickly befriended Sara and seduced her with his knowledge of the occult. In a subsequent meeting, Adolfo met the couple together, completely ignoring Gilberto's offer of a handshake and focusing his attention exclusively on Sara.

Later, an anonymous phone call informed Gilberto that Sara was dating someone else. The drug dealer went into a jealous rage and confronted Sara. She denied the allegations but he broke off the relationship anyway.

Sara then turned to Adolfo for comfort. He told her that he knew that Gilberto would break up with her as he had seen her future in a tarot card reading. Adolfo proceeded to "comfort" Sara by seducing her but their physical relationship would not last.

"Sara started dating Constanzo until she found out he was gay," Gavito said. "She said 'no problem'. But he told her what was he was involved in and she introduced him to the Hernandezes. So it was Sara that was the one that connected all of this people together."

Adolfo wanted a meeting with the leader of the Hernandez family, Elio, and Sara arranged for that to happen. Adolfo saw that he could influence drug dealers with his dark magic and earn a nice living for himself. Charming Elio Hernandez would be step one toward that goal.

When Sara returned to the college, her classmates noted that her demeanor changed significantly. Sara obsessed on witchcraft and magic in every conversation. She wanted to argue on the merits between good and evil.

Sara eventually left her studies behind and Adolfo welcomed her into his growing cult. He christened her as "La Madrina", the Godmother. He himself was "El Padrino", the Godfather.

WHO WAS ADOLFO CONSTANZO?

Adolfo was born in Miami, FL on November 1st, 1962 by a fifteen year old girl who would subsequently have three children by three different men. His mother, named Delia Aurora Gonzalez, had her son blessed by a Haitian priest who practiced *palo mayombe*, a form of witchcraft that owes its origins to the Congo but was passed down to Cuba and Puerto Rico with the settlement of slaves.

The boy's mother was excited when the Haitian priest pronounced that her six month old child was "chosen" and "destined for great power."

Delia moved the family to San Juan, Puerto Rico shortly after his baptism. Adolfo's childhood was steeped in the teachings of the dark imaginings of his mother. She taught him the rituals of her bizarre religion even as he became an altar boy at the local Catholic church.

When Adolfo was ten, his mother moved her growing family back to Miami. They once again met with the Haitian priest and young Adolfo began an apprenticeship under the man.

A MOTHER FROM HELL

Adolfo's mother Delia was arrested over thirty times. Her rap sheet included shoplifting, passing false checks, grand theft and child neglect.

Her punishment, however, was always lenient and she was never sentenced to anything more than probation. She attributed her ability to escape jail stints to the spells she cast under *palo mayombe* and she passed down this belief system to her son.

A true tenant from hell, she left every apartment she stayed in a vandalized mess. Delia left the walls and floors bloodstained with the remains of animals that she sacrificed. Living in a section of Miami known as the Coral Park Estates, Delia lorded over her neighbors in a reign of terror. Earning her reputation as a witch, Delia was vindictive with anyone who dared inspire her wraith. Neighbor Elena Menendez found a dead goose on her door step with its head wrapped in a red handkerchief. Carmen Reiganda opened her door to find a decapitated chicken on her porch after her son had gotten into an argument with Delia.

Mother and son left a legacy of fear behind in the small Miami neighborhood and the majority of the people were afraid to talk about them.

"Everyone here is worried (Adolfo)will come back to get them for talking," said one man. "I've completely protected my house, and if they come by, I'll blow them away."

LIKE MOTHER, LIKE SON

Adolfo inherited both his mother's religion and criminal ways. He indulged in Miami's gay bars during his teens and earned a living through petty theft. He found school to be a burden and was only interested in learning about black magic. The boy barely graduated from high school and dropped out of junior college after one half-hearted semester.

He continued to obsess about witchcraft with his Haitian priest mentor. They formed a team to rob graves at midnight to stock the priest's lair with dead bodies. They created voodoo dolls and sprinkled blood over them to curse people that crossed them.

The philosophical tenets of *palo mayombe* laid the foundation for Constanzo's future drug dealing endeavors. The belief system places no value judgments on the individual, there is no "good" or "evil" magic. Criminals familiar with the practice used it to protect them from the law but the Haitian priest had a solemn warning for his young student.

"Let the non-believers kill themselves with drugs," the priest said. "We will profit from their foolishness."

By the age of fourteen, Delia became convinced that her son had psychic abilities. Adolfo claimed to have predicted that President Ronald Reagan would be shot by John Hinckley. Adolfo had a murky vision for his own future, however, as he was arrested twice for shoplifting in 1981, including one incident where he tried to steal a chainsaw.

Two years later in 1983, Adolfo had sworn his allegiance to *Kadiempembe*, the name for Satan in *palo mayombe*. The Haitian priest gave Adolfo his blessing as the boy vowed to worship evil in return for financial gain. The priest initiated Adolfo into the fold with a ritual scarring as he took a knife and sliced arcane symbols into the body of his young student.

"My soul is dead," Adolfo said at the end of the ceremony. "I have no God."

BEGINNING OF A CULT

Blessed with good looks, Adolfo landed a modeling gig in 1983. He traveled to Mexico City for a photo shoot and earned some extra money telling fortunes with tarot cards in the city's dangerous Zona Rosa (Spanish for "Red Zone", a strip of prostitutes, bars and drug dealings.)

The trip to Mexico netted him his first cult followers which included Martin Quintana Rodriguez, Jorge Montes, and Omar Orea Ochoa. Adolfo had affairs with Quintana and Orea, wherein he would be the "woman" or the "man" in the relationship depending on his mood.

In 1984, Adolfo moved his base of operations to Mexico City permanently. He lived with both Quintana and Orea, engaging in nightly homosexual ménage à trois. He began offering his psychic services around the city, developing a reputation for seeing into the future and offering *limpias.* These were ceremonial "cleansings" for those who thought they were cursed by life or wanted some enemies taken care of.

Adolfo kept records of his dealings with the townfolk and his journals revealed that he had thirty-one regular customers. Some of his patrons would pay up to $4500 for one single ritual. Adolfo gave his customers a menu in which they had a choice of sacrificial animals to choose from. Roosters went for $6, goats $30, boa constrictors $450, zebras $1100, and African lion cubs were $3100.

Adolfo began to target the more successful drug dealers in the area. He would help them schedule shipments and customers based on his own alleged "visions". He would charge exorbitant fees for his "magic" to make dealers and their henchmen invisible to police and remain bulletproof against would-be assassins.

Most of the drug merchants had upbringings that paralleled Adolfo's in that their parents were poor peasants who believed in the supernatural. They made for easy dupes for the charismatic cult leader who had one dealer pay him over $40,000 for his supernatural blessings over a period of three years.

Adolfo always delivered, however, as he realized that at such prices his magic would have to be just that, a magic show spectacle. On one occasion he and three of his followers broke into a Mexico City graveyard and excavated numerous graves for bones. His reputation grew as his stage show became more elaborate. He was soon entertaining physicians, business men, fashion models and a host of transvestite cabaret singers. In a bizarre twist, there were several high-ranking police officials that joined Adolfo's cult. The most notable was Salvador Garcia Alarcon, a lead narcotic investigator and Florentino Ventura Gutierrez who was the head of the Mexican branch of Interpol.

The devotion of these individuals clearly went beyond mere bribery or charm. It soon became apparent that they worshiped the young

Satanist as he led them on a tour to all of the pits of hell he could dream up.

A year later, Ventura would introduce Adolfo to the infamous Calzada family, arguably Mexico's biggest drug cartel at the time. Letting his charisma do the work for him, Adolfo won the gang over with an elaborate ritual and they repaid him for his blessings of "magic". By 1987, Adolfo had amassed enough cash for a luxury condo and a slew of high-end cars which included an $80,000 Mercedes-Benz.

"Constanzo made these people believers," Gavito said. "I think it could happen to anybody. Most of these kids came from good families And they're already involved in moving narcotics. So I think it was easy to graduate into the cult part of it. Because they saw the wealth and they saw the power that Constanzo had."

Adolfo liked to push the envelope, however. Not satisfied with his payments from the drug dealers, he disguised himself as a DEA agent and relieved a Guadalajara dealer of his cocaine stash. He sold the coke through his police connections for a $100,000 profit.

As the stakes rose, so did Adolfo's need to have more over-the-top rituals. It was during this time that he began incorporating human sacrifice into his ceremonies. His callousness in both torturing strangers and his closest friends scared both the dealers and police officials into remaining on his good side if they could.

The Calzada drug cartel bought into Adolfo's act hook, line and sinker. The simple minded drug dealers attributed their continued prosperity and survival to his magical powers. Adolfo sensed his influence over the family and realized that he had became a necessary "good luck" charm to them. In the spring of 1987, Adolfo called for a meeting with the heads of the Calzada family. He demanded to become a full partner in their drug dealing enterprise.

The Calzada family rejected the notion immediately.

Adolfo, however, realized that if he was not going to be given power then he would take it.

On April 30th, 1987 Guillermo Calzada Sanchez and six members of his family disappeared under suspicious circumstances. They were reported missing on May 1st with the authorities discovering remnants of what looked like a Santería ceremony at Calzada's office as they found as melted candles and bones scattered about. A week later, mutilated remains washed ashore on the Zumpango River. The police trolled the river and recovered the seven bodies. All of the corpses showed signs of severe torture: fingers, toes and ears were removed, genitals slashed, a spinal column was excised from one body, two others had their skulls opened with their brains missing.

The body parts of the Calzada drug cartel were now part of Adolfo's growing *nganga* or cauldron, a large iron kettle where he stirred up his "witch brew."

His primary drug competitors now eliminated, Adolfo believed that he was growing stronger in his dark magic and began setting his sights on bigger targets.

The Hernandez family became next on his to do list. Adolfo set up a meeting with the powerful Elio Hernandez through Sara who had been dating his son. Adolfo had received word that the Hernandez cartel had dissension in the ranks and were becoming more vulnerable to competing drug families.

During their talk, Adolfo convinced Elio of the efficacy of the *palo mayombe*. He seduced him with the idea of taking his enemies and sacrificing them to his Satan God. In return, Adolfo promised that his family and drug enterprise would be blessed by the dark forces, that they would become invisible to police and bulletproof.

"Give me fifty percent of the profits," Adolfo said. "And I'll control things."

THE BELIEVERS

In 1987, Adolfo became obsessed with a film called the *The Believers* which starred Martin Sheen and Jimmy Smits. It was a movie that showcased the Santeria and voodoo possession and Adoflo saw himself in the characters. He sought to replicate what he saw on the screen into his own rituals.

"It is not at all surprising that Constanzo and Sara Aldrete were infatuated with the movie *The Believers*," said occult researcher Carl Raschke. "The magical practitioners in the film are portrayed as insuperable and almost all knowing."

Adolfo saw the film as validation for what he was doing, specifically conjuring up the spirit realm to aid him in his crimes. Sara, on the other hand, used the movie as a recruiting tool for prospective members.

"[There is]...a story making the rounds that tells of the night Aldrete persuaded three male friends to screen a video of *The Believers*," Rolling Stone magazine reported. "After the film, say the students, Aldrete stood up and began to preach in strange tones about the occult. 'They had been drinking and they just thought she was trying to be spooky,' said one of the students who knew the boys. 'but they look back on it now and think she must have been serious.'"

THEY MUST DIE SCREAMING

Adolfo's thirst for more power and wealth required that his rituals become more specific and gruesome. He moved his cult to a place called Rancho Santa Elena which was about twenty miles away from Sara's hometown of Matamoros.

On May 28th, 1988, Adolfo murdered a drug dealer named Hector de la Fuente and a farmer named Moises Castillo in sacrifices to his demon God. Not satisfied with the level of sadism he achieved in those killings, he then tortured and mutilated a transvestite named Raul Paz Esquivel. Paz was a former lover of one of Adolfo's original followers, Jorge Montes. The level of torture was extreme as they dismembered Paz's body, turning him into a bloodied pretzel. Paz' dismembered body was then left on a city street only to be discovered by school children.

Sadism and torture became foremost on Adolfo's mind as he sought new ways to increase his depravity. Invariably, he would sodomize his victims before their death, giving them one last indignity. Blood and guts fed his cauldron where Adolfo turned the "stew" like a modern day witch. He believed that the devil he worshiped would be more pleased if his sacrificial victims suffered as much as possible.

"They must die screaming," Adolfo intoned to his followers.

THINKING BIG

On August 10th, 1988, rival drug dealers kidnapped Ovidio Hernandez and his two year old boy. They wanted revenge for being ripped off on an $800k deal.

Adolfo, feeling the need to show off the efficacy of his *palo mayembe*, kidnapped a random stranger off the street and brought him to the ranch. They tortured the man, offering him as a sacrifice to their Satanic God while praying for the safe release of the Hernandez family member and his son.

Three days later, the dealers released Hernandez and the boy without any ransom money being exchanged. The Hernandez family gave full credit to Adolfo and his use of witchcraft.

He had them under his spell...

NO SAMPLES FOR YOU

Three months later, a 35-year old ex-policeman turned cult member named Jorge Valente de Fierro Gomez was caught using drugs, stealing from Adolfo's stash.

Adolfo decided to make an example out of his follower as he didn't want any of his members to partake in the drugs. The ex-cop became yet another sacrificial offering to *Kadiempembe*.

On Valentine's Day of 1989, Adolfo's group captured three competing drug dealers and tortured them to death. They dismembered the bodies and added them to the gruesome brew. A week later, another sacrificial victim had been kidnapped but the man put up such a lengthy fight that the group was forced to kill him before he could be tortured. The followers continued their quest to acquire victims. They came upon a 14-year old boy and killed him before realizing that the teen was a cousin of Elio Hernandez.

The boy cried uncontrollably as Adolfo's henchmen had the knife to his throat. Adolfo decided that the boy could be added to the brew because he was too sad. If they sacrificed the boy, then the demon god would be sad. So they killed the boy and went out to the streets to find another young boy.

Adolfo did this because he wanted to acquire the boy's youth. When he wanted "youth" he would have a young boy kidnapped and sacrificed. When he wanted "strength", he would have a strong man kidnapped and dismembered into his brew.

SPECIAL BLESSING NEEDED

By this time, Adolfo had amassed over 800 kg of marijuana that his followers had stolen from another gang. He thought he needed a special blessing to ship the large amount across the Rio Grande. His followers kidnapped another stranger off the streets but Adolfo was not satisfied with the level of sadism they had achieved in torturing the man. He felt that his demon overlord, *Kadiempembe ,* would require a new benchmark in torture and pain.

"Bring me someone I can use," Adolfo said. "Someone who will scream."

He also wanted someone smart, someone who had medical training. He instructed his followers to keep their ears out and find an American college student who was going into the medical field.

The next morning, his followers brought in a young college student named Mark Kilroy.

SPRING BREAK HORROR

Matamoros had been a popular hangout for college students on spring break for decades. Students would come upon the small Mexican city looking to let loose in the uninhibited foreign soil that offered prostitution, nudie bars, booze and drugs.

By March of 1989, however, the town had over sixty unsolved disappearances over the course of three months. Unfortunately, this did not deter the usual contingent of American collegians from descending upon the town and enjoying the nightlife.

Mark Kilroy was one of those tourists.

A popular high school student, he played on the basketball and golf teams. He served on the student council and graduated 14th in a class of 210. He initially enrolled at Tarleton State on a basketball scholarship but transferred to the University of Texas after two years, giving up his basketball aspirations to concentrate on his pre-med courses. He was, by all accounts, an upstanding young man.

His father, Jim Kilroy, recalled that when his son was in high school, he would sometimes go to Mark's bedroom to make sure he was studying. He would find the young man reading his Bible instead. "What do you do?" Kilroy asked as he recalled the memory of his son. "He needs to study. But do you go in and tell your son to quit reading the Bible?"

Mark had trekked to Mexico for the spring break with three friends who were all his former classmates at Santa Fe High in Texas.

"The whole semester," a friend recalled. "That (the trip) was all we talked about."

They spent the night enjoying the Mexican food and drinking. They chatted with some girls visiting there from Kansas then returned without incident to their rooms at the Sheraton Hotel on South Padre Island over 20 miles away.

The second night would be quite different. They spent the evening drinking and then around 2 o'clock in the morning they began walking toward the bridge which connected Matamoros with the Texas border town where they had parked their car. Two of Mark's friends walked ahead while Mark and Bill Huddleston lingered about twenty feet behind. Huddleston briefly stepped into an alley to urinate. Mark waited on the street.

When Huddleston came back onto the street he could not find Mark anywhere. There were no signs or sounds of struggle.

THE ABDUCTION

Four of Adolfo's followers had kidnapped Mark. They had been driving a red pick up truck along the main drag of Matamoros, tailing the group unnoticed.

When they spotted Mark alone, they offered him a ride.

"They all had badges that said 'state police,'" Gavito said referring to the fact that Adolfo's followers disguised themselves as cops. "They all had jackets that said police on them. They had red lights in their car. They ran around Matamoros like they were police officers. When (Mark) went off to use the bathroom that was the perfect time. They went up to him, they badged him, they put him in a car, they told him he was under arrest for being drunk. They drive down about two blocks. They pull over, they all get out, the policemen, the guys 'acting' as policemen. They wait for the other car to show up. (Mark) jumps out and starts running."

Mark Kilroy ran for two blocks. The Constanzo crew chased him down yelling "freeze".

"(Mark) being the well educated boy that he is," Gavito said. "Who was brought up to respect the law, when he heard the word 'freeze', he stopped. He was half a block from getting back on the main drag where there was two thousand kids partying. And he stopped, they handcuffed him, they threw him back in the car, they took him back to the ranch. They tied him up and they put him in the back of the Suburban."

He was given food and told he would not be harmed.

Twelve hours later, however, he would be sacrificed.

Kilroy was the only American kidnapped by the cultists. He also came from an affluent family including an uncle that worked for the U.S. Customs Service. His father was a chemical engineer and his mother a volunteer paramedic. The family were devout Catholics, active in their local church.

The response from from the public was immediate. There was a $15,000 reward for information leading to his return or the arrest of his kidnappers.

Yellow bows graced the churches of his hometown and beyond. Dozens of people joined the search for Kilroy, with hundreds of flyers being handed out around the town. San Antonio Mayor Henry Cisneros lobbied Mexican authorities to find the young man.

"I had worked with the Mexican police for over twenty years," Lt. George Gravito recalled. "Best cooperation you've ever had in your life. All of a sudden, I ran into a wall. No cooperation. The state police was telling us that (Mark) was involved in narcotics. But they wouldn't tell me where they're getting the information. This guy was corrupt. What we're meeting with right here on the border, one day you're investigating a crime in Brownsville, Texas and tomorrow morning you're investigating it in Matamoros, Mexico. It's not your jurisdiction and you have to know how to move around. You can't step on the wrong toes because they're gonna kick you out of the country."

The Matamoros police interrogated over one hundred known criminals in the area in the search for Kilroy. They beat their legs with clubs and sprayed soda water mixed with hot sauce into their nostrils.

They came up with nothing.

ONE MORE SACRIFICE

Adolfo had used the sacrifice of Kilroy in his mind to ensure the safe shipment of his marijuana. But now, he thought he needed yet another special sacrifice to his palo mayombe overlord.

Adolfo decided to target Sara's former boyfriend, Gilberto Sosa.

On March 28th, 1989, Sosa became the cult's final sacrifice as the marijuana made its way across the Rio Grande on April 8th.

Adolfo's alleged psychic abilities would fail him, however, as his depraved empire would soon come to an end in a way that he didn't foresee...

PURE LUCK

The police drew no leads for two weeks until they came across a "happy accident" on April 10th of that year...

"We were lucky," Gravito recalled. "What helped us in this investigation was, we had been working on some narcotic cases. DEA Brownsville had been working real close with *un commandante* in Matamoros. That *commandante* was Juan Benitez Ayala. He was the head of the federal police assigned to the Matamoros area. This man, Juan Benitez Ayala, I'll say was about five feet tall. But he probably stood about eight foot tall. I mean when this guy walked in anywhere people were scared of him. He worked and that's all he did.

"You didn't see him in bars. You didn't see him in restaurants. And the reason he didn't go to bars or restaurants, one, he was afraid someone might put something in his drink and kill him. The guy was taking down some powerful people in Mexico and we went to talk to him."

"I told him we got this problem with this state police guy, he says these kids were involved in narcotics, and I assure you that they weren't. We had helped them on some cases, we had busted some big people (because) we had shared some information. So he put his people to work. And every time we had a lead, we'd call him, we'd go over there, we'd kick doors down, you know, you don't need a search warrant, the search warrant IS the federal police and nobody gets in your way."

The Mexican police had erected roadblocks and began a random drug roust in areas of Matamoros unrelated to the Kilroy disappearance. They had a policy of targeting only the low level runners and leave the heads of the drug operations alone.

Serafin Hernandez was the epitome of the low-level drug dealer. He was the twenty year old nephew of Elio Hernandez and a well known trafficker. During this drug roust, Serafin came across the police checkpoint and was followed. He unknowingly led the officers to the innocuous looking cattle ranch. A shabby looking corral marked the front with a tar paper and wood shack that stood in the rear of the winding, unmarked road.

It was Rancho Santa Elena, the home of Constanzo's cult.

The police waited a week and returned en masse, arresting both Serafin and another dealer named David Serna Valdez. The interrogations began and the two dealers proved to be cocky witnesses. They claimed they were "protected" by supernatural powers, of course referring to the spells that Adolfo had cast.

Inside, the police found a horror chamber beyond the imagination of any snuff film. The 15x25 foot shed was saturated with blood and smelled of rotting flesh. They found human brains, hair, teeth and skulls. Some spines had been crafted into necklaces. Scattered around were machetes and white votive candles in a box that bore a picture of *Our Lady of Guadalupe*.

The press nicknamed Rancho Santa Elena as the "Devil's Ranch."

"I thought in my twenty two years of law enforcement I had seen everything," a Texas deputy said. "I hadn't. As we drew near, you could smell the stench...blood and decomposing organs. In a big, cast iron pot there were pieces of human bodies and a goat's head with horns."

MAKING THE CONNECTION

"About two o'clock in the morning I get a call from *el commandante*," Gavito recalled. "We found (Mark) he said. 'You found (Mark)? You kidding?' he said no. We found (Mark). Where? He said he's buried in a ranch outside of Matamoros. I asked him how? Or who? He said there was a caretaker that also lived near the ranch. When he arrested Serafin, he picked him up too, the caretaker, but he didn't file charges against him. But he kept him under house arrest and the caretaker saw a picture of (Mark) on top of the table. And he pointed to it and said 'I know that boy'. 'How do you know him?' 'I was feeding him. I was giving him bread. I untied one of his arms so he could sit up and eat' because they had him tied to the back of a Suburban."

El Commandante then began interrogating Serafin. Without prompting, Serafin began offering information on how he knew Mark Kilroy, admitting that he was the one who kidnapped him.

"This guy was volunteering all of this information," Gavito said. "I mean usually in Mexico you have to go, you know, I guess its something you have to know when you get arrested, that they're going to torture you to get the truth out of you. But I've never heard of anybody just confessing this easily as Serafin. And we kinda talked a little bit and the name Constanzo had come up on his investigations. Serafin had said that they had kidnapped (Mark) because the *Padrino*, Constanzo, wanted somebody who was studying medicine because they were doing some kind of witchcraft."

"They were going to use Mark's brain to give it to this pot that they had. And I didn't understand what he was talking about and I said did you have to torture this guy and he said 'no, this guy (Serafin) thinks that bullets do him no harm and the police can't hurt him he thinks that this guy, this Constanzo is gonna come in here and take him out of here."

"It's our religion," Serafin said. "Our voodoo."

George Gavito recalled that during Serafin's confession he repeatedly made reference to the aforementioned film, *The Believers.*

"I remember I didn't understand what he was telling me," Gravito said. "I said, 'Is it Santeria?' And he said, 'Yeah, yeah, Santeria, voodoo, man.' And then he kept on saying, 'The Believers, The Believers, The Believers.'"

"Elio made [Serafin] Garcia a priest, but Garcia didn't really know what he was practicing because all he had on his mind was the movie."

Serafin told the authorities about El Padrino, the Godfather, as being Adolfo Constanzo. He revealed the details of Adolfo's ritual of African magic, palo mayombe. "Adolfo ordered the slayings," Serafin said. He revealed that the Godfather had tortured and sodomized his victims before killing them. They would then mutilate the bodies and harvest the organs for his witches brew.

SCENE OF THE CRIME

Serafin was brought back to the Devil's Ranch with Ayala and Gavito, both police officials not expecting the level of depravity they were about to investigate.

"We asked him where the body was," Gavito recalled. "And he said 'which body?' Just like that. 'Which body?' 'Man,' El Commandante says. 'Man, if you're playing games with me' and he got pissed off. And he (Serafin) says 'hold on, which body you want?'"

"'What do you mean, which body!'" El Commandante screamed.

"There's a bunch of bodies out here," Serafin said. "Which one do you want?"

"What do you mean?"

"Yeah," Serafin began walking through the corrals. "There's one buried here, there's one buried there."

"How many?"

"I don't know."

"Where's Mark?"

"Over there in the corner."

"Where?"

"I don't remember exactly," Serafin said as he started walking to a corner of the corral. "But I think it is where that wire is."

The police looked down and saw a coat hanger half-buried in the dirt.

"Why a coat hanger?"

"Oh, because Constanzo wanted to make a necklace," Serafin said. "With Mark's backbone. So after we killed them and everything we ran wire through his back, through the spinal cord, so that later on we could just come and get it out and he could make a necklace."

Disgusted and angry, Benitez-Ayala handed Serafin a shovel, forcing him to dig up the body of Mark.

During the dig, Serafain revealed that Constanzo had killed Mark with one machete slice to the back of his head. He began revealing more details of other killings, matter of factly and without feeling. At one point he even asked if the police we're going to order food because he was getting hungry.

El Commandante Benitez-Ayala became enraged. He took out his Uzi and fired the weapon into the air out of frustration.

"You don't think bullets can hurt you?" he asked Serafin.

"No," Serafin replied.

El Commandante then began emptying his entire clip.

"That's when the kid's eyes opened up," Gavito recalled, remembering how frightened Serafin became. "I mean his eyes opened up when he heard that sound, I mean it freaked us all out because we didn't realize what was going on. He (Serafin) went from being a believer to being a disbeliever pretty quick. He went back to being a normal person."

Serafin suddenly snapped out of his brainwashed state.

"I don't know why they got us to do this," Serafin said.

"All of a sudden it was 'why' they got us to do this," Gavito said. "It just changed."

His body unearthed, Kilroy's skull had been split open and his brain removed. The police then found a nearby shed wherein they located Adolfo's *nganga*, a cast-iron cauldron that was stained with blood, body parts and numerous sticks, the "palos" of *palo mayombe*.

Inside the kettle were spiders, scorpions and the brain of Kilroy. His brain had been boiled in blood over an open fire along with a turtle shell, a horseshoe, a spinal column and other human bones.

FAILING MAGICAL POWERS

Adolfo was surprised at the reaction to Kilroy's disappearance. He was used to his killings not gaining any notoriety at all. Even after the fact, three of the unearthed victims have never been identified and only a handful were reported missing.

The next day, all hell break loose for the cult members. Four members of the Hernandez family were arrested and the cash from their big marijuana sale was confiscated. The police began unearthing bodies from the ranch on April 11th, finding more bodies in a nearby orchard.

Feeling the heat, Adolfo went on the run with Sara, and his two lovers Martin and Omar. A Hernandez family hit man named Alvaro De Leon Valdez, nicknamed "El Duby", came along as well.

Adolfo's first instinct was to go to Miami where he could be with his mother. He decided to stay travel to Mexico City, however, using the homes of followers and friends of followers to hide.

The gruesome discoveries made the rounds in tabloid television. Geraldo Rivera produced a segment on the murders. There were false sightings of the cult being reported in the United States. Adolfo was claimed to have been seen in Chicago where people mistakenly labeled him as part of the Windy City Mafia. Sara was reportedly seen skulking around schools throughout various border towns, threatening to kidnap and kill ten white kids for every one of her followers that were jailed in Mexico. There was a church located in Pharr, Texas that was burned down after rumors that some if its members were connected to Adolfo's cult. Serafin Sr, a drug dealer and follower of Adolfo, was found and arrested.

The national news did little to shed light on the whereabouts of Adolfo, however. They successfully hid from sight as if their Devil God had swallowed them up and welcomed them into hell...

BETRAYAL IN THE CARDS

Adolfo did a tarot card reading on April 18th, 1989 and supposedly foresaw a betrayal among his followers. He knew that any of the many low level drug runners could have ratted out Serafin Sr and he now looked at his followers with a suspicious eye. He kept a gun close by and did his best to avoid sleep. His paranoia led to angry outbursts against his acolytes.

"They cannot kill you," he warned. "But I can."

The Commandante, Juan Ayala, meanwhile, took the threat of Constanzo's *brujeria* (witchcraft) very seriously.

"He flew in his own brujo (male witch), to take care of him and to take care of all his agents," Gavito said. "To make sure there was not 'bad vibes'. And not only that, but to help him in the investigation. To find out what was the best way to catch Constanzo. He (the witch) told Benitez, 'you wanna catch him? Burn their hut! Burn their nganga! Burn where they were worshiping.'"

"So we got out there one Sunday morning. Took one Mexican television station to cover it because he wanted Constanzo to see this. The brujo puts gasoline around it. They light it up and it starts to burn and we sit there while the whole thing burns to the ground."

Adolfo watched the scene on television as Ayala had hoped. His screen police sifted through what was left at the ranch. He then went into a rage inside the small hideaway apartment, smashing furniture and flipping over the couch for starters.

"He felt raped," Gavito said. "He felt that we had invaded his privacy. That we had done something we shouldn't have. He started losing it."

MOVING ON

Adolfo made one last move with his followers as they found an apartment on Rio Sena in Mexico City.

Sara, finally realizing her life was in danger or needing to now play the role of the victim since the authorities were no doubt closing in, made a handwritten note. She threw it out the bedroom window in the hopes that a Good Samaritan would come along and find it.

The note read:

Please call the judicial police and tell them that in this building are those that they are seeking. Tell them that a woman is being held hostage. I beg for this, because what I want most is to talk—or they're going to kill the girl.

A stranger walking by picked up the note but kept it to himself, thinking it was a joke. Upstairs, however, Adolfo plotted his next getaway move.

"They'll never take me," he said.

MORE RANDOM LUCK

A few days later, police arrived on Rio Sena and began going door to door looking for a missing child. Adolfo saw them from his window and began opening fire with his Uzi not realizing that they were not looking for him.

Over one hundred eighty-police men almost immediately. A fiery battle ensued which lasted almost forty-five minutes. Surprisingly, the only person injured during the crossfire was an officer who was struck by Adolfo's first barrage.

According to Sara, Adolfo ordered his own killing, telling El Duby to shoot him and his right hand man, Martin Quintana Rodriguez.

"He lost it," Gavito said. "He turned on the stove. Put the money on the stove. Started burning money. He started throwing coins out. Just lost it."

"He went crazy, crazy," said El Duby. "He grabbed a bundle of money and threw it and began shooting out the window. He said everything, everything was lost. No one's going to have this money."

"He wanted to die with Martin," Sara said.

Adolfo soon realized he was trapped. He handed his Uzi to El Duby.

"He told me to kill him and Martin," El Duby said. "I told I told him I couldn't do it, but he hit me in the face and threatened that everything would go bad for me in hell. Then he hugged Martin, and I just stood in front of them and shot them with a machine gun."

The police entered the apartment with guns raised but Adolfo and Martin were already dead, their bodies slumped together in a closet. The three remaining cult members, El Duby, Orea, and Sara were captured.

Over twenty rounds were found in autopsied body, possibly indicating that the Mexican police had continued to shoot him port-mortem.

THE TRIALS

El Duby's case was open and shut. He had confessed to the two murders and had no reasonable defense. Sara, however, was a tad different as she initially proclaimed to be a victim but knew too much of the cult's ins and outs to not be considered an accomplice.

After the shootout, fourteen cult members in total were indicted for murder. In August of 1990, El Duby was convicted of the killing of Adolfo and Martin, getting a 35-year prison term. Juan Fragosa and Jorge Montes were convicted to 35 years for the killing of Raul Esquivel.

Omar Orea, one of Adolfo's lovers, died of AIDS before going to trial.

Sara had been acquitted of Adolfo's slaying but was sentenced to a six year term for her criminal associations. She maintained her innocence throughout, stating that she never practiced the *palo malembe* but a "Christian Santeria."

Showing a calm demeanor during her interrogations, Sara expressed sorrow for the murders of Kilroy and the other victims.

American law officials saw Sara as having a split personality. They knew that in private, Sara would lose her "charming aspect" that she revealed when she knew the television cameras were on. She reverted into another self, talking with relish in describing the cult's rituals.

"I would say she has three personalities," a Mexico City attorney general said. "One personality comes out and faces the cameras and denies any involvement in the human slayings, another emerges when she talks to police and the third one comes out when she talks to herself."

American Customs agent Oran Neck spent several days in Mexico City assisting the local police. "Sara has kind of lost touch with reality," Neck said after he questioned her. "Her dual personality is coming up pretty strong right now. When you talk to her without the TV cameras there, she's pretty truthful."

"She gives a lot of data with great detail to investigators. It seems like when the cameras come on, she kind of reverts back to this nice, young, clean-cut kid from Texas Southmost College."

"When the cameras were there, she was real nice," Lt. George Gravito said. "When she was with us, she was the same ol' witch."

SARA'S SENTENCE

"If I had known it (the cult) was like this," Sara said. "I wouldn't have been in it."

Six years after her criminal association sentence was up, Sara was tried again and convicted of several of the murders at the cult's headquarters. She is now serving 30 years in prison.

During an interview with SFGate, Sara claimed that she was tortured by Mexican police after her capture. She said she was stripped, blindfolded, hung upside down, beaten, had her toenails pulled out and was burned inside her vagina in and out. She claims the burns were so severe that a doctor told her she'd never have children.

She also remembers the police shoving her hands into Adolfo's autopsied body at the morgue.

They yelled at her to pull out his heart.

"There is your devil," they mocked. "There is your prince. Kiss him. Kiss him."

The Mexican authorities have denied these claims.

"The witch deserves everything she got," Lt. George Gavito said.

Mark Kilroy's parents have said they have forgiven her but do not want her released. "You have to control a mass murderer," said Jim Kilroy. "What are you going to do? Let her loose and have her murder other people?"

Even after the convictions, some murders from the time period have remained unsolved. Between 1987 and 1989, there were 74 unsolved ritual murders in Mexico City. 14 of these involved children. Adolfo's cult is connected to 16 but there has been no evidence to connect them to the rest.

"We would like to say, yes, Constanzo did them all," prosecutor Guillermo Ibarra said. "And poof, all those cases are solved. And the fact is, we believe he was responsible for some of them, though we'll never prove it now. But he didn't commit all of those murders. Which means someone else did. Someone who is still out there."

ELLISHIA ALLEN, KILLER

A Crime Where Everyone Is a Victim

Has an alcoholic committed themselves to a life choice for which they must pay any penalties that, as a result, come their way? Or are they subject to a compulsive behaviour disorder which should be taken in mitigation against any consequences that end up at their door? Perhaps, just as importantly, is this a question about which the authorities care?

These are questions that will trouble anybody connected to the sad case of Ellishia Allen and Karl Bloxham. Ellishia was a pretty normal, everyday girl who had a problem with drink. It led her, to murder and a fourteen year life sentence in a British jail.

And her victim was a boyfriend, Karl, whom she dearly loved. His death took away a good, kind man who loved his killer as much as she did him.

Meeting Among the Burger Wrappers

Ellishia Allen had met Karl Bloxham in the unlikeliest of places. Both were undertaking community service for alcohol related misdemeanours in 2008. Karl had been convicted of driving under the influence of alcohol. This is a dangerous – potential deadly – crime. One that is irresponsible in the extreme. But Karl had learned his lesson and was taking his punishment on the chin. Ellishia's felony was more bizarre. She had been on a flight and spent the journey drinking. Then, in an extremely inebriated state, she had gone to the toilet where she had lost her hand bag.

Most of us will, at one time or another, made use of the facilities in an aircraft and will know that the tiny cubicles do not lend themselves to the misplacement of personal items, certainly not ones as large as noticeable as a hand bag. It was evidence of the drunken state Ellishia was in that this is what happened to her. Or, at least, that is what she thought.

When we are drunk, our inhibitions race away along with our ability to make rational decisions and keep our emotions in check. Unfortunately for Ellishia, and for those nearby, when she became drunk she did not quietly shrink into her shell, as some do. She had a tendency towards losing her temper and becoming aggressive. This is what happened on the plane, to such an extent that she could not be controlled.

So worried were the cabin crew that the plane had to divert to the nearest airport and make an unscheduled stop so that the drunken young woman could be safely removed and given a chance to sober up. These days, with our sensitivity towards aircraft crime, such behaviour would almost certainly result in a custodial sentence. But Ellishia was young, with a clean record, and she was sentenced to community service rather than time behind bars. Her judge, Charles Kemp explained his decision to suspend any custodial sentence. 'Your conduct on that plane was an absolute disgrace,' he admonished, before continuing to say that it was...'outrageous in terms of the interference with cabin crew who have responsible jobs to carry out.' The flight she had caused to be diverted was one flying home from Tirana, Albania in August 2007. She was just 21 at the time.

She had crawled, lashing out her arms and legs, along the floor towards the cockpit. On her arrest at the airport, she had spat at police. (Later that year, she was again arrested for spitting at two police officers.)

She was a part of a team who were cleaning litter from the roadside. An unpleasant but necessary task. For a glamourous girl like Ellishia, the punishment was doubly degrading. But she accepted her punishment and got on with the work. As a part of the process for ensuring that those serving their sanction got on with the job, and avoided the pitfalls of re-offending, it was common practice to 'buddy up' those identified as most at risk of re-offending with someone who had simply strayed once from the straight and narrow.

Karl Bloxham was such a man. He was a natural leader among the group cleaning the roadside, and the officer in charge of the team saw a chance for his positive influence to do even more good. He paired together Karl with Ellishia, little knowing that the older man and glamour model would find more in common than sweeping the hedges and bushes clean on Nottingham's litter strewn thoroughfares. Karl was eleven years older than the partner on whom it was intended he would keep an eye. But any older brother care he displayed soon turned to mutual friendship, then physical attraction, then love. Before long they had moved in together, a not untypical couple living in a not untypical working class home in a working class town.

Living In the East Midlands – A Region of Gentle Extremes

For those who know their British Isles, the region identified as the East Midlands does not quite fit. Britain likes to define itself with neatly caricatured identify. The far south east is the 'Garden of England', albeit a garden these days filled with speeding lorries heading to its ports rather than fishing gnomes.

The west country is a rural idyll, with rolling hills and spectacular beaches. London is the cosmopolitan centre of Britain, and annoys the remainder of the country as a result. Wales is home to mountains and choirs and dead industry; the north is the site of the industrial revolution, and many of its buildings are still stained by the smoke of factories from Victorian times. Further north and the land becomes spectacular once more, and the people are known for their thriftiness and blunt speaking.

In the middle of it all lies the appropriately named Midlands, the industrial heart beat of the country. Strong local accents remain, the people friendly and the economy uncertain. But then there is the East Midlands. Sweeping countryside dotted with honey stoned cottages; huge estates and hunts that belong in the 19th century sit alongside some of the most troubled towns in the country.

Nottinghamshire is home to the spectacular Sherwood Forest, home of the (probably) fictional Robin Hood. The astonishingly beautiful peak district lies on the doorstep. Yet Nottingham and its surrounding towns are in a constant state of failed regeneration. Industries come and go. Once the centre of lace manufacture in the world, who today covers their table top in fine, intricate linen? And even if our granny does, that lace lasts forever. Next mining came and went, collieries opened, then became exhausted. The cost of recovering the coal seams beneath the land became just too expensive.

Hucknall – A Most Unremarkable Town

Hucknall is one such Nottinghamshire town. A town with a long, distinguished past once served by no less than three railway lines. Now it sits a dormitory town for the large but unmemorable sprawl that is Nottingham. While they can't take away the views – particularly the fine ones down to the River Trent – much else is in continuous decline. The town centre was recently pedestrianised, but it's small shops are disappearing, leaving behind charity shops, fast food joints and the occasional bookmakers.

But if Hucknall, like much of the rest of urban East Midlands, is a largely mundane place, it is not a hotspot for crime; there are drugs on the street, but not at every corner. Burglaries, muggings, assaults are more commonplace than we would like, yet not at epidemic proportions. It has a small number of famous inhabitants – Lord Byron is buried there, DH Lawrence grew up nearby. But not an exceptional number.

Many of its 32000 inhabitants make the short eleven mile drive to nearby Nottingham for work, which also offers most of their social activities. Similarly, anything more than a stock up on groceries is likely to promote a trip to the city's shops. The nearby M1 gives quick access to more interesting locations.

In fact, for the very mixed region that is the East Midlands, Hucknall is remarkably ordinary. It was also home to Karl Bloxham and Ellishia Allen.

They lived in a quiet residential street called Spruce Grove. While spruce trees are only noticeable by their absence (no doubt, once one flourished before making way for progress, remembered only by old people who used to play in the field that once was when they were kids, and a small sign celebrating the name sitting low on a wall.

Spruce Grove is a cul de sac. 1950s semi-detached houses line three quarters of the road. None of the honey coloured stone that enhances much of the East Midlands countryside here, instead red brick overlooks the narrow lane. There are no garages, and little room for off road parking. The road is too narrow for two cars to pass, so vehicles sit half on and half off the road. At one end, low bungalows sit, built it seems in the same decade.

This is social housing, or at least, homes designed as such. No doubt, the low bungalows were designed for the elderly, for those who fought in the first war, or lost love ones in it. The larger semis are there for the young families of the baby boomer generation.

Then, as those with a bent for history will know, along came Margaret Thatcher and her plan that everybody should own their own home. Houses like those in Spruce Grove were sold off at an astonishingly cheap rate. Now the road is largely privately owned, with council owned properties dotted among the homes. There is no obvious way to tell the two apart.

Local authority housing, particularly that built in the years following World War II, might look a little faceless on the surface. The trend at the time was for uniformity. But they do benefit from being spacious. That meant that some of the homes along Spruce Grove had been converted from one (for English standards) reasonably sized house into two small flats. The inhabitants of these really did live on top of each other, and it was one such apartment that Karl and Ellishia shared.

Spruce Grove is, in brief, a typical working class home in a typical small East Midlands town. From the outside, the homes appear well kept, the gardens tidy and the hedges trimmed. Fifty years ago wives would clean the front steps at least once a week. It is not the kind of place were murders take place.

A Mostly Happy Relationship Wrecked By Mental Illness

Ellishia and Karl enjoyed a close and loving relationship. Mostly. They moved in together in 2011 and much of their four years together was marked by mutual affection. But both liked a drink, and Ellishia in particular found that once she opened a bottle, she found it hard to leave it unfinished. Then, once the alcohol started to take effect, a drink would turn into a binge, and her behaviour would become unpredictable as a result. During these times, according to a neighbour, their relationship became 'volatile and unpredictable.'

And it was not just alcoholism from which Ellishia suffered. Compulsive personalities are usually compulsive in more than one direction. In Ellishia's case, her problematic mental health saw her suffer from bulimia and anorexia as well as alcoholism. These combined to lead her to a diagnosis of an emotionally unstable personality disorder.

Evidence of this came to the surface from time to time. At one point, she was convicted for assaulting a police officer. Another time, prior to her relationship with Karl beginning she posted a worrying and violent comment on her Facebook page.

'...is beatin the shit outa sum1 n findin great pleasure in it! all that tension inside, u say where the recovery in that? Oh theres gud recovery I say, oh I do. oh year its someone else but luvin it! feel great nw thinks its time for round 2! I feel mint nw! lol x' she wrote with low regard for grammar or clarity of expression.

But struggling to put a sentence together is of less concern to the violent one to the post. It is further evidence of a strong temper which hid behind her usually steady temperament.

Her school years were challenging to Ellishia. She struggled academically, and her compulsive nature and quick temper led her into trouble from time to time. Post education, she used her stunning and contemporary good looks to get work as a glamour model. Her long blonde hair and attractive face taking her far enough to get published in Nuts Magazine.

Nuts Magazine was a publication of its time. First published in 2004 it is best described as a very mildly pornographic 'lads' magazine aimed at the young male 18-30 market, although it was probably most often to be found hidden under the mattresses of fourteen year olds. It was a magazine in which sexual content was alluded to rather than explicitly shown. A combination of changing social attitudes to the overt presentation of women as sexual objects, contradictorily matched by increased availably of on line porn saw the magazine's sales drop from a peak of more than 300000 copies in 2007 to a sixth of that by the time it closed in 2014. Perhaps the key decision that led to its downfall was the decision by popular high street supermarkets to insist that the publication be hidden behind an opaque cover if it was to remain on its shelves.

Nevertheless, to become a model displayed in Nuts meant that, for someone happy to pursue that line in her career, Ellishia had achieved a level of relative success.

Breaking Point

On July 29th 2015 matters had reached crisis point. Even the weather that day reflected the state of Karl and Ellishia's relationship – general warmth and calm was punctuated by heavy, sometimes violent, showers. Mutual love and affection was still present, but when Ellishia succumbed to drink, she changed. And those changes were becoming increasingly common place. Karl held enormous sympathy towards her conditions – her poor mental health as well as her alcoholism. But there was only so much support he could give if she was unable, or unwilling, to take steps to open herself up for treatment.

Another argument ensued, and Karl opted to go to his local pub for a drink with friends from work. While he was there, the decision that he had been putting off making raised its head once more. This time, he felt that their relationship really had reached the end of the road. He texted

Ellishia, telling her 'It's over.' Ellishia responded as erratically as might be expected given her fragile and intoxicated state.

She alternately told him the he would not do it, and told him that she had thrown his clothing out into the street. Karl told her that he would be round to collect his belongings, and once there, sought to take immediate necessities, planning to return at the weekend to gather up the remainder of his possessions.

Reports from neighbours suggested that tempers blew quickly. Loud thumping sounds were heard from their home, their dog was barking as though in distress or aggravated by what was going on. Doors were heard slamming and Ellishia was heard to shout 'Karl, please don't leave me.' Another neighbour reported hearing a male voice, presumably that of Bloxham, shouting, 'Stop, you're hurting me.'

Ellishia has always been reasonably open about what happened that night. Only a small number of facts are debated. She seized a knife with a long, 12 cm blade, from their kitchen draw, and she stabbed him through the heart with it.

Realising the horror of what she had done, she immediately called the emergency services. Her panicked conversation with the operator was recorded, and replayed in court.

'I've just stabbed my boyfriend,' she exclaims. 'He's dying in front of me. I've just stabbed him. He was calling me names.'

She goes on to say: 'I've got a mental health problem. I just grabbed the knife and I've just stabbed him in his heart. I didn't know where I was stabbing him, and I've stabbed him to death.' Her panic increases: 'He's dead...his eyes are open and he's dead. He's not moving...and I stabbed him.' The time was 9.52 pm, more than an hour before pubs close. It seems unlikely that Karl was intoxicated. An ambulance was despatched, and paramedics worked on the wounded man for thirty five minutes, but they could no revive him. He was pronounced dead at the hospital later that evening.

An Unsympathetic Trial

As to whether there were any mitigating circumstances through a sense of threat from Karl, the judge at her September 2016 trial in Nottingham Crown Court was clear. 'I'm absolutely sure you picked up a knife and used it because you were angry because Mr Bloxham decided to leave you,' said Judge Gregory Dickinson QC, before sentencing Ellishia to life, with a minimum term lasting fourteen years.

This was despite pleas from her counsel Peter Joyce, QC, explained that his client suffered from multiple disorders, and met every criteria required for a diagnosis of having an emotionally unstable personality disorder.

'At the time of the offence she was suffering from a number of recognised medical conditions,' he tried to explain. 'It is plain tat she was utterly stricken by remorse for what she had done.' His words, though, fell on deaf ears.

Detective Inspector Andy Bateman worked the case for Nottinghamshire Police. After Ellishia had been sentenced, he said: 'I feel enormously sorry for the parents of Karl Bloxham and for his sister and friends.'

He went on to add 'I'm also conscious that he had children from a previous relationship and I I'm very sorry they have been deprived of him.'

Dt. Insp. Bateman concluded: 'Today's events won't bring him back but I would hope that Allen is able to complete treatment in prison and have time to reflect upon her actions.'

Karl's family shared the sentiments expressed by DI Bateman. Kylie Petrice is Karl's sister. She said: 'I miss him. I regret that I did not tell him enough that I loved him.'

Their father, Ted, felt understandably even more strongly. Explaining that he had not only lost his son, but his best friend, he explained the depth of distress from which he and the family were suffering. 'We have a life sentence ourselves that will never go away,' he told the court in his victim impact statement.

Alcoholism – A Disease Not a Lifestyle Choice

Back in 1985, a study by Steele and Southwick confirmed what anyone who had been a victim of alcohol abuse knew only too well. That alcohol affected social behaviours. It makes us more aggressive, more adventurous and less inhibited. Much less, though, was known about why that occurred.

However, Steele and Southwick hypothesised that alcohol instilled a greater effect on a person's behaviour when the brain was stimulated by the requirement for a social response. This can be understood through the analogy of one of those fairground pirate ships which rise and fall and twist and turn. Sit in the middle of the ride – be sober – and the pulls and pushes can be felt, but induce less of a reaction. Sit on the edges and those same forces play much greater havoc with our equilibrium – as they would were we under the influence of alcohol.

When we look more into the scientific explanation for alcohol addiction, it becomes even clearer that this is a medical condition to which some people are more clearly prone, not a lifestyle choice that people can take or leave.

Bearing in mind that medical understanding of the brain is still extremely basic, but expanding all the time, we already know that alcohol is addictive to the brain for a number of reasons. Firstly, it triggers the release of dopamine, which is a chemical which makes us feel happy and contented. (Something which, in the case of a person such as Ellishia who already suffers from other mental health conditions inducing feelings of inadequacy and stress, would be very welcome.) Secondly, it increased release of endorphins, the brain's natural pain killer. Scientists believe that the brain craves the release of this particular chemical, and once it experiences a trigger, it craves the return of that trigger.

Doctor Jonathon Crick is a consultant psychiatrist at Edinburgh University. His research suggests a further reason why certain people become addicted to alcohol. This reason is one especially linked to a person such as Ellishia.

'Chemicals are only part of the picture,' he explained to the BBC. 'They do not explain it (alcohol addiction) fully.'

He goes to explain this. 'For example, there are people who have a nervous, anxious disposition.' (Something from which Ellishia clearly suffered, as evidenced by her anorexia and bulimia). 'If they start to use alcohol as a tranquiliser, that can become addictive.'

Dr David Ball works for an addiction charity. He is able to explain the nature of addiction further. 'People can have a genetic predisposition to alcohol addiction, but it can't be triggered if people aren't exposed to alcohol in the first place.' Unfortunately, Ellishia was exposed to the drug, and from a young age. While that is true of many, many people who do not develop addictions to alcohol, nor fall to extreme behaviour under its influence, it seems clear that such a reaction is a medical outcome, not a chosen one.

Other research now suggests that the issue of addiction is a genetic one. Research suggests that people whose parents struggled with alcohol abuse are ten times more likely to suffer themselves than the population as a whole.

When Political Expediency Matters More Than Medical Understanding

It seems that such knowledge did not influence the judge in Ellishia's case, and nor was it considered by either the police or the crown prosecution service. Then again, their respectively struggling reputations are built more on success in court than necessarily justice.

However, while the position of the victim and their loved ones must always be considered simple imprisonment seems a blunt and unsophisticated tool to address a complex personality disorder. Perhaps that might change in the future. More probably it will not.

This is a particularly sad case. While it seems certain that the blame for Karl Bloxham's death lay firmly at the door of his girlfriend, Ellishia Allen, she was a woman in distress. Her mental health problems meant that the normally reliable woman underwent periods where her behaviour became extreme. Whatever treatment Ellishia received to help her address her periodic instability clearly had minimal impact.

Her situation was aggravated by alcoholism. But that is an illness which requires treatment, not criticism. Of course, murder can never be justified, or excused. Yet it can be explained. The judge in her case seemed sure that she killed her boyfriend in a fit of jealous anger. Seemingly, her mental state was not considered problematic enough to offer mitigation. That is a harsh decision, one which may well become increasingly rare as understanding about mental disorder and alcoholism makes it was through the long dusty corridors to the attention of politicians and the judiciary.

Then again, there are many more votes in blaming alcoholics, than in treating them. So it may be that political pressure is never fully moderated by medical understanding, and judges such as Judge Gregory Dickinson will continue to punish rather than treat. Looking back on reports of the case, they are sadly few. Ellishia's conviction, Karl's death and both of their suffering are modern tragedies. But an alcoholic former glamour model murdering her boyfriend in their unexceptional home in their unexceptional town doesn't sell many papers. There is a short section of a US documentary episode examining the case. It seems as though the producers found the East Midland accent too much to master, as their actors sound more Australian than guttural Midlanders. A few newspaper reports and major TV news reports still linger online, but they tell us very little beyond the most basic of facts. None of the stories offers us anything original.

And there lies the sadness of this case. The personal tragedy of two people, the impact on their families, is deemed not worthy of attention when there are more newsworthy items to report and glamorise. That, in its way, is another tragedy highlighted by this case.

Balancing the issues caused by mental illness against the importance of protecting the population is an impossible conundrum – one which leads to suffering on all sides. Ellishia Allen, Karl Bloxham and both of their families would attest to that. Vehemently.

SERIAL KILLER JUANA BARRAZA

MARCUS MOORE

Juana Barraza is perhaps the most famous serial killer in all of Mexico's history. Authorities have attributed the death of up to 48 elderly women in Mexico to Juana, and she was found guilty in 2008 of several murders and was sentenced to a total of 759 years in jail for her crimes. Referred to as Mataviejitas, or Little Old Lady Killer, Juana's killing spree and the subsequent police investigation, became national news in Mexico in 2007 and 2008, and led to widespread pressure on the police department to solve the series of crimes against the nation's most vulnerable members of society.

Background

Juana Barraza, or Juana Dayanara Barraza Samperio, was born on December 27, 1958 in the small rural town of Epazoyucan, Hidalgo, located north of the nation's capital of Mexico City. Her father, Trinidad Barraza, was a local police officer and her mother, Justa Samperio, was a prostitute. Juana's mother left her father shortly after Juana's birth to begin a relationship with a married man named Refugio Samperio, was was Justa's stepfather during her childhood.

Juana reportedly suffered from a difficult and violent childhood, living with an extreme alcoholic for a mother. She was illiterate as a child and was often physically and emotionally neglected by her mother. She would later claim that her mother sold her to a strange man named Jose Lugo when she was only twelve years old for just three beers; the man sexually assaulted Juana repeatedly and she became pregnant with a boy. Juana would eventually have a total of four children, although her oldest son died in a robbery attempt at 24 years old.

Prior to becoming famous for her role as a serial killer, Juana was a relatively little-known wrestler who participated in the amateur circuits of *lucha libre*, a famous form of Mexican wrestling that involves the use of masks and significant amounts of stage drama. During her career as a wrestler, she performed under the stage name *La Dama del Silencio*, also known as The Silent Lady in Spanish.

While Juana toured the country as a part of the amateur wrestling circuit in the 1980s and 1990s, she turned to stealing and burglary in 1995 after birthing her fourth child. In 1996, she began robbing elderly people with a friend of hers, setting up a pattern of targeting the elderly that would last throughout her entire criminal career. The two burglars would dress in all-white scrubs and pretend to be nurses in order to gain their victim's trust and access to their homes.

Crimes

Juana's profile as a serial killer was that she consistently targeted elderly women, in their late 60s or older. Many of her victims lived alone and had little contact with local relatives or a strong social circle. Juana would typically befriend the victim, then lure them to their home or a quiet place where she would bludgeon them to death with a heavy object or strangle them with an extension cord that she carried on her person, usually robbing the victim once they were dead.

Juana used several different methods to gain her victims' trust. She would often cruise the streets of poorer neighborhoods, looking for elderly woman who were by themselves and struggling with bags of groceries or other household items. She would then offer to help the elderly women up their set of stairs to their apartments, where she would the kill her victim. Juana would also frequently pose as a government official, complete with an ID badge and government application forms. She would claim that she was going door-to-door to help pensioners apply for their benefits in order to gain their trust and access to their home. She frequently used phone cords, extension cables, tights, or a stethoscope to strangle her victims.

It is suspected that Juana's first victim was Maria de la Luz Gonzalez Anaya, who was murdered on November 25, 2002. Juana gained access to her apartment, likely in order to rob the elderly woman, but ended up killing Maria Gonzalez after the woman made disparaging comments about Juana, angering her and leading to her strangling the victim in a fit of rage.

Several years into her career as a serial killer, Juana Barraza began a romantic relationship with Jose Francisco Torres Herrera, a taxi driver known as *El Frijol*, or The Bean. Together, the two continued her killing spree and began by targeting Carmen Camila Gonzalez Miguel, an 82-year old wealthy woman in Mexico City. While the pair did successfully kill Carmen and escape, this murder led to a widespread police response and investigation into the existence of a serial killer in Mexico City. Carmen Gonzalez was the mother of Luis Rafael Moreno Gonzalez, a well-known and powerful criminologist. Her death led to increased police patrols, a public information campaign, and a collaboration with French investigators, who had recently detained *The Monster of Montmartre*, a prominent French serial killer.

Police Investigation

During the early stages of the investigation into a potential serial killer, the chief prosecutor for Mexico City, Bernardo Batiz, publicly said that he thought the killer had "a brilliant mind, quite clever and careful" and that he suspected the killer was adept at gaining the trust of their potential victims prior to killing them. Several officials believed that the killer was posing as a government benefits counselor who established trust by offering to help the victim secure government benefits like health care and welfare.

There was an odd coincidence which confused the police working on the case and led to detectives investigating misleading information that ultimately delayed Juana's capture. Early on, the police noticed that at least three of the women killed by Juana owned a copy of the *Boy in Red Waistcoat*, a famous painting from the 1700s by French painter Jean-Baptiste Greuze. For some time, police were convinced that the presence of this painting had some important bearing on the case and why the victims were chosen; but, ultimately it became clear that the presence of the painting was mere coincidence and that the police department's focus on this "evidence" was misplaced.

Police were able to determine through their investigation and subsequent in-person interviews that Juana was clinically classified as a psychopath: she did not feel any pain or remorse for actions, and thus had no moral qualms about her actions and their effects. Psychologists say that Juana associated the elderly women that she preyed on with her mother, believing that her actions were a net good because she was removing evil people from the world. Her lack of empathy, combined with her engaging persona and false identity as a government worker, allowed her to gain these women's trust in a small amount of time.

Despite the rash of killings in Mexico City in late 2005 and early 2006, the local police department consistently dismissed any theories of an emerging serial killer and called out such ideas as "media sensationalism." However, police did begin to take reports of a serial killer seriously in November 2005, when they received several witness statements reporting that the killer wore women's clothing, leading them to suspect that the serial killer was actually a transvestite who posed as a woman to gain access to, and trust from, his victims. On one particular occasion, the killer was seen living a victim's house wearing a red blouse.

Once the police department finally did launch a full investigation of the killings, their first action was to launch a city-wide raid of all of the areas frequented by transvestite prostitutes, since they mistakenly believed at that time that the killer was a transvestite who dressed as a female in order to gain the trust of his female victims. A reporter for La Jornada, a popular newspaper in Mexico City, would call the series of raids "ham-fisted" unproductive.

In addition to detaining and questioning all of the city's known transvestite prostitutes, the police also began visiting the local morgue to check fingerprints. They believed that the killer may have committed suicide and that they need only verify the identity of one of the corpses to close the case. This belief would quickly prove to be incorrect.

Despite initial fumbling by the police department and an investigation predicated based upon incorrect assumptions about the killer, the case would soon break open in a very public way. On January 25th, 2006, a suspect was seen fleeing from the home of the now-deceased Ana Maria de los Reyes Alfaro, an 82-year old women living in the Venustiano Carranza section of Mexico City. Ana Alfaro was strangled to death with a stethoscope by Juana Barraza. Luckily for the police, Alfaro was a landlady and one of her new tenants was arriving at her home as Juana attempted to flee the scene of the crime. The tenant nearly bumped into Juana as she rushed out of the building and was the first to see Reyes Alfaro's body. He immediately called the police and was able to provide the description that led to Juana's capture.

In a surprise to both the police, national media, and public, the suspected killer was actually Juana Barraza, a 48 year old amateur wrestler, and a woman that many people would mistake for a kindly grandmother; here was the famed Mexico City serial killer, and the nation was shocked.

Police investigators were initially drawn to the idea of a transvestite serial killer because of composite sketches and witness statements that described the serial killer as a masculine-looking woman. Given these statements and the fact that the vast majority of serial killers are men, they police department completely ignored the possibility that the killer could actually be a "masculine-looking woman," as opposed to a man dressed as a woman.

Despite this initial confusion, police quickly realized that Juana looked remarkably similar to the police sketches that had been composed from witness statements. The more that police learned about Juana, the more that her role as the serial killer made sense. Police initially thought that the killer had to be a man or male transvestite because of the sheer amount of strength required to strangle someone. They thought that it was impossible for a woman possess that much physical strength; however, Juana was no ordinary woman. She was a professional wrestler reportedly capable of bench pressing 200 lbs for multiple sets of ten, a significant sign of strength in any person.

Furthermore, her use of the stethoscope to kill her last victim was in line with witness statements, which had described a government worker with short, dyed-blonde hair and a mole on their face, carrying a stethoscope, benefit forms, and a government ID card.

Once detained, police were quickly able to connect Juana to at least ten other murders using her fingerprints. Mexico City's chief prosecutor at the time, Bernardo Batiz, would tell the media that "Fingerprints match in 10 murder cases, as well as one attempt." In addition, police investigators found several trophies related to the killings in her home, including cutouts of newspaper articles discussing the killings (despite the fact that she is illiterate). Juana admitted to killing Ana Alfaro, but said that she had initially visited the elderly woman's home in order to secure work during laundry and that she killed the woman out of "anger," and not because of any premeditated reason.

Trial

Juana Barraza began her trial for murder in spring 2008, with prosecutors claiming that she was responsible for up to 40 killings over the previous six years. While Juana admitted to killing Ana Alfaro, claiming that she murdered the elderly woman out of anger because she resembled Juana's abusive mother, she claimed that she was innocent of all of the other charges levied against her.

Despite her claims of innocence, Juana was sentenced to prison for 759 years in March 2008, after being found guilty of 11 separate murder charges and an aggravated burglary charge. Given that federal sentences in Mexico are served concurrently and legally the maximum sentence a person can receive is 60 years, it is likely that Juana will die in prison. However, she will be eligible for parole in 2058, when she is 100 years old.

Suspected Victims
Robbery
1995-2001

Juana is suspected of robbing a large, unknown amount of victims during this time period.

Murder

2002

November 24th: Maria de la Luz Gonzalez Anaya (64 years old)

2003

March 2nd: Guillermina Leon Oropeza (84 years old)

July 25th: Maria Guadalupe Aguilar Cortina (86 years old)

October 9th: Maria Duadalupe de la Vega Morales (87 years old)

October 24th: Maria del Carmen Munoz Cote de Galvan (78 years old)

2004

February 20th: Alicia Gonzalez Castillo (75 years old)

February 25th: Andrea Tecante Carreto (74 years old)

March 20th: Carmen Cardona Rodea (76 years old)

March 26th: Socorro Enedina Martinez Pajares (82 years old)

May 24th: Guadalupe Gonzalez Sanchez (74 years old)

June 25th: Esthela Cantoral Trejo (85 years old)

July 1st: Delfina Gonzalez Castillo (92 years old)

July 3rd: Maria Virginia Xelhuatzi Tizapan (84 years old)

July 19th: Maria de los Angeles Cortes Reynoso (84 years old)

August 31st: Margarita Martell Vazquez (72 years old)

September 29th: Simona Bedolla Ayala (79 years old)

October 24th: Maria Dolores Martinez Benavides (70 years old)

November 9th: Margarita Arredondo Rodriguez (83 years old)

November 17th: Maria Imelda Estrada Perez (76 years old)

2005

January 11th: Julia Vera Duplan (60 years old)

February 10th: Maria Elena Mendoza Vallares (59 years old)

April 13th: Maria Elisa Perez Moreno (76 years old)

April 14th: Arturo Patino Barranco (74 years old)

April 19th: Carolina Robledo (79 years old)

April 20th: Ana Maria Velazquez Diaz (62 years old)

June 17th: Celia Villaliz Morales (78 years old)

June 29th: Maria Guadalupe Nunez Almanza (78 years old)

July 5th: Julia Vargas (64 years old)

July 5th: Mario Cruz Flores (84 years old)

July 20th: Emma Armenta Aguayo (80 years old)

August 9th: Emma Reyes Pena (72 years old)

August 11th: Carmen Sanchez Serrano (76 years old)

August 15th: Dolores Concepcion Silva Calva (91 years old)

September 28th: Maria del Carmen Camila Gonzalez Miguel (82 years old)

September 28th: Guadalupe Oliver Contreras (85 years old)

October 18th: Maria de los Angeles Repper Hernandez (92 years old)

2006

January 25th: Ana Maria de los Reyes Alfaro (84 years old)

Juana' Public Response

Juana has repeatedly denied that she is a serial killer, although she has admitted to at least one murder. During her first appearance in court for her trial, she stated "I only killed one little old lady. Not the others. It isn't right to pin the others on me." When she was later asked about her motive for the sole killing that she took responsibility for, she simply said, "I got angry."

Juana has maintained her innocence throughout her trial, verdict and during her current stay in prison, remarking at her verdict, "May God forgive you and not forget me." She has vowed to appeal all but one of the charges she was found guilty of, claiming that her sole killing was a crime of passion against Ana Alfaro on the day she was caught.

TWISTED SISTERS : THE TRUE STORY OF REGINA AND MARGARET DEFRANCISCO

CHAPTER ONE

Regina and Margaret DeFrancisco are two sisters convicted of first degree murder.

On paper, the two sisters look like two girls you would see at a church social.

In school, both were good but not great students. Margaret was the pretty one. She would get all of the attention from the boys but return little interest.

Margaret was a student at Jones College Prep School, a selective public institution that is considered one of the top high schools in Illinois.

A little on the shy side, Margaret had a quick wit and sense of humor. Sweet-looking and pretty, she had avoided any kind of trouble throughout her young life. Her early photos suggest, however, that her subtle smirk was a couldn't contain the narcissism that was growing within.

"You would look at Margaret and see right through her," one of her neighbors said. "It was black, like was nothing there. She didn't seem like she had depth, like she had compassion."

Regina had a love for animals, particularly ponies. She rode horses and in her words, "never lost a show."

Regina was also the more extroverted of the two, wearing her emotions on her sleeve. She could mouth off and had a chip on her shoulder. She also had a thing for 'bad boys', seeing them as a reflection of herself.

"A lot of girls get turned on by the 'thug life,'" forensic psychologist Marnie Clark said. "The DeFrancisco sisters definitely fit that mold. They were not out to play Mrs. Cleaver when they grew up. They were attracted to the gang lifestyle. They thought the drama was exciting."

The girls were raised by a single parent, Nora DeFrancisco. Nora raised the two sisters and their brother Joey in the Pilsen neighborhood of Chicago. Their father, Augie DeFrancisco was a small-time burglar and convicted drug dealer who had no involvement in the girl's childhood years. Their maternal grandfather, Gilbert Smith, was a former Chicago cop who was fired from the force in 1960 after admitting that he was "friendly with certain burglars."

Growing up in Pilsen, however, the girls could not avoid rubbing shoulders with gang members. They became enamored with gang culture, learning who fought against who and what the names of the gangs were. There were the Latin Counts, Kool Gang, Villa Lobos, Bishops, among many other offshoots. The girls knew what streets signified what gang members' territory and memorized their hand signals.

"Chicago is simply rife with gangs," Clark said. "It is inescapable, even to those in the more affluent communities. There is still a choice, however. For whatever reason, the DeFrancisco sisters were drawn to the 'thug life'. To a young person, it looks 'cool'. They are the classic examples of young women who could not see the big picture and thought the thug life was something worth aspiring to."

The two sisters, with their striking brunette looks, could not help but come into the cross hairs of the local gang members. They began wearing dark lipstick and teasing their hair out. Margaret would get a tattoo on her belly. Regina would have the letter "R" tattooed on her leg as well as a drawing of a heart just above her breast. They would hang out on street corners and in front of the local liquor store, chatting up the neighborhood 'gangstas'.

"The changes in their make-up and dress signified the changes in their personality," Clark said. "They grew bored during their time at prep school. Even ashamed. They did not want to see themselves as nerds and hated that aspect of themselves. Starting in eighth grade, it was time to start rebelling. By the time they reached high-school, the thug life was part of their persona. Dark make-up. Tattoos. Hanging out with gang bangers. Alcohol and drugs. But most important, they wanted all the drama that came with that kind of life. Who is out to get who, who dissed who and who shot who became their modus operandi in life."

Grandfather Gilbert, however, had seen this all before as a Chicago cop. He feared that the girls, particularly Regina, would become ensnared by the street gang culture. He tried to obstruct this from happening and found Regina a job with a local periodontist. He figured if he kept the girl busy with school and work it would keep her away from the idiots on the street.

Regina, however, did not have the emotional maturity to see the light. She showed up late for her first couple of shifts then she was fired.

But she had started dating a man named Johnny Rivera, a known member of Chicago's notorious "Latin Kings" street gang. Rivera had a rap sheet as long as "War and Peace" as well as more aliases than a Russian spy

Regina would learn how to package and deal drugs at the foot of Johnny. She would watch him put the cocaine into plastic bags, measuring it out by the ounce. They would drive around town and Johnny would introduce her to his customers, watching as he conducted the deals. The secret handshakes and secret lingo all became apart of Regina's world.

Officially crossing over from innocent prep school girl to drug dealing girlfriend, Regina lived a double life. She did manage to get a part-time job doing data entry work for a local law firm and had enrolled in the local junior college (Harold Washington).

Margaret was getting into trouble as well. Her grades in high school were slipping as she would sneak out at night to be with friends. She would often come to school looking "disheveled" according to one teacher who thought she looked like a child whose parents were going through a divorce.

And there was trouble on the home front.

Neighbors would report hearing the girls fighting with their mother on a daily basis.. The two girls were out of control with no father figure to put them in line. Nora would berate Regina whenever she would act up in school or get arrested and the girls would yell back.

In private, Nora would refer to her daughters as "the bitches".

Things would come to a head when Regina would get arrested for selling cocaine to an undercover cop. A single mom already strapped for cash as she had to support three children on her own, Nora was livid as she paid Regina's bail.

"How are you going to pay me back?" .

"I don't know!"

"Do you know how much it costs to bail you out of jail!" Nora screamed. "You are going to pay me back. You're going to pay me back every penny!"

CHAPTER TWO

"She needs money," Margaret said, her voice full of concern.

"How much?" Oscar asked.

"One thousand dollars. Can you help us out, baby?"

That was the scene set for the twenty-two year old Oscar Velazquez in June of 2000 as he spoke to the sister of his current teenage crush, Regina DeFrancisco. He spotted Regina around the neighborhood of Pilsen and quickly fell for her dark Irish-Italian good looks. Showing off his brand new Z28 Camaro, he chatted up the girls before he asked Regina out for tacos. The two began going out but Regina didn't like him...at first. Then she realized that he had some money and was all too willing to spend it on her.

"Oscar wasn't the typical guy that Regina would go for," Clark said. "Regina liked the 'bad boy', the thug. Oscar wasn't in street gang culture. He had immigrated from Mexico and actually had a real job, earning his living the old fashioned way as a truck driver. If anything, Regina would see someone like him as a sucker, someone who she could use."

Still, Regina was what Oscar wanted. He persisted in calling her, asking when he could see her again.

"He's a creepy guy," Regina told her sister, Margaret as her cell phone rang. She looked at the caller ID. Yep, it was Oscar.

"But maybe you can get some money from him?"

"Here, you talk to him," Regina said handing the cell phone to Margaret. "Just make up some baloney that I'm in jail or something."

"What?"

"Get rid of him. Tell him I need bail money."

"Hello, Oscar?" Margaret answered the phone.

"Yeah," Oscar said. "Who is this?"

"It's Margaret," she said, sounding as if she was trying to stifle tears. "Regina is in jail. She's locked up."

"What?"

"They put her in jail for something she didn't even do. They want one thousand dollars. One thousand dollars to bail her out."

Margaret smiled like a devil at her sister.

"I can help," Oscar said.

"No," Margaret said, sniffling. "It's too much."

"It's for your sister."

Oscar would persist in his willingness to help out, however. Margaret played him like a violin, agreeing to meet with Oscar to take his hard earned money.

"Oscar gave Margaret the money in the hopes of scoring points with the sisters," Clark said. "He thought that by being 'nice' and bailing them out of trouble they would find him attractive. Instead, it just fueled their contempt for him. These girls liked thugs. Bums. They cared little for Oscar's chivalry."

Regina would not use the money to pay back her mother, however. She would give the money to her real boyfriend, Johnny, who bought an "old school ride" car with Oscar's money.

Oscar would call Regina over twenty-four times during the next five days wanting to know what happened. He began to feel like the sucker he was.

He had a wife and kids in Mexico. But here in Chicago he fell for the brown-haired beauty and became all too willing to be her patsy.

"Oscar was playing with fire," Clark said. "He just didn't realize how far gone the girls were in terms of narcissism. He didn't see the fact that they didn't even see him as a human being. All he saw was batting eyelashes and pretty faces. He was totally smitten with Regina despite the fact that he had a wife and kids back in Mexico. Here he was, in Chicago, where he was free from the responsibilities of family. He could have a little fun and if he had to spend some money to do it, so be it."

CHAPTER THREE

The two sisters were surprised at how easy it was to extract money out of Oscar. With one fake phone call, they had one thousand dollars cash to their name.

"They were both attractive girls in the neighborhood," Clark said. "They were young, looking up to gang members and drug dealers for the power they had. But the girls realized that they had their own power. The power of budding sexuality that could make men do what they wanted. They could trick men into doing things for them with a future promise of sex."

Oscar continued to call and it would be only a matter of time before he would be confronted with the truth that he had been lied to. The girls had to construct a plan to get rid of him.

"I have an idea," Margaret said, picking up the cell phone and calling their fifteen year old friend, Veronica Garcia.

"Need your help," Margaret said as Veronica picked up.

"For what?" Veronica asked.

"I need a gun. Can you get a gun?"

"A gun?"

"Can your boyfriend get a gun?"

Veronica, like the DeFrancisco sisters, was enamored with street gang members. She had a boyfriend who could obtain whatever you needed, drugs or guns.

"Why?"

"We're going to stick up and rob Oscar," she said.

"You're not going to kill him are you?"

"We're just going to scare him a little," Margaret laughed.

Veronica did as she was asked, getting a gun from her boyfriend and heading straight over to the DeFrancisco sister's home.

"Nice," Margaret said, looking the pistol over, closing one eye as she looked through the cross hairs. "So where we going to do this?"

"Right here," Regina said, waving her hands around the living room.

"No way," Margaret said. "If the neighbors complain about us screaming and yelling then they're going to hear a gunshot. Duh."

Regina looked around the home. The basement door caught her eye.

"We'll lead him down there," Regina said, leading her sister down the basement steps. "Nobody can hear anything down here. The noise will be drowned out."

"Here," Margaret said, removing some blue tarp from the shelf. She spread the material down on the basement floor in front of the steps. "We can't leave any blood stains."

"Check you out," Regina laughed. "Miss Perry Mason."

Margaret laughed as she flattened out the tarp, placing it in a perfect line with the basement stairs. "Okay," she said, walking halfway up the steps. "So if we shoot him from here," pointing her forefinger into a gun. "He'll fall straight down there."

"Perfect."

The two sisters giggled and gave each other fist bump.

"Here is where the disconnect took place," Clark said. "They had embraced an environment and a culture where there were a lot of faux tough guys. Guys who said they would commit violence but for the most part it was all talk. The girls took it literally. At no point did they realize the gravity of what they were doing. They wanted to be 'gangstas', they wanted to be seen as 'hard'. They didn't have the maturity or the experience to realize that all of those 'gangstas' that they look up to are in jail. They didn't see Oscar at all. He was less than human. Something that is used, discarded and desecrated when it is no longer of use."

CHAPTER FOUR

Oscar was surprised that Regina finally called him back.

"Hey," she said, her teenaged voice soft and inviting.

"You're out of jail?" he asked.

"Yeah," she said. "I really appreciate what you did for me. That was really sweet of you."

"No worries," he said. "I need my money back. Been calling you like crazy."

"I'm sorry, I've just been busy."

"Yeah, I understand. But I need my money back."

"I was wondering if there was some other way I can pay you back?" she said in a sensual tone of voice.

"Like?"

"Like, I know you think my sister is hot, right?"

"What's that got to do with anything?"

"It is something we've been thinking about," she said. "But if you're not cool with it, it's okay."

"Not cool with what?"

"We were wondering if," Regina giggled. "If you can come over for a threesome."

Oscar couldn't believe his luck. He had heard of white girls being freaky, he just didn't think he would ever be able to experience it himself.

Naive to their plan, he rushed over and parked his car outside their mother's home in the South Side of Chicago.

He knocked on the door and was greeted by Margaret and Veronica Garcia, a friend of the two sisters. He didn't see the .38 caliber semi-automatic pistol had in her back waistband.

"Does anyone else know you're coming over?" Margaret asked.

"No," Oscar mumbled, shrugging his shoulder.

Margaret nodded her head and let the young man in. He saw Regina step into the room holding a bin of dirty laundry.

An awkward silence ensued followed by even more awkward smiles. The two sisters fed off each others willingness to go through with the plan. Even if one of them had second thoughts, they would be deemed "soft" by the other.

They had to go through with the murder.

Both women looked over at the young man with come hither looks. Regina said nothing as she opened the basement door and walked down.

"You go with Regina," Margaret said smiling.

"Right," Oscar said, his heart pounding in anticipation as he followed her down.

Oscar heard Margaret's footsteps behind him. What he didn't know was that she had a gun pointed at the back of his head.

When he reached the bottom step, she pulled the trigger.

The young man died instantly, falling face first in the tarp.

"Holy shit!" Margaret said. "I had no idea it would be that fucking loud. It doesn't sound that loud on TV."

Margaret came down the stairs. She kicked Oscar in the head hard, sending more blood spraying across the floor and wall.

"Nobody heard," Regina said as she knelt down and began rifling through Oscar's pockets.

"What the fuck was that?" Veronica said, calling down from the top of the basement steps.

"Did you see that? " Margaret asked. "He fell down like a baby!"

The sisters took out his wallet which had over $600 cash. They took his cell phone then ripped off the sterling silver chain from his neck.

"What the fuck happened?" Veronica said, her voice trembling as she came down a few steps.

"We shot his ass," Margaret said. "He's dead. Look at that shit, he's bleeding through his ears."

"Why did you do it?" Veronica screamed. "Why? Oh my God!"

"Shut the fuck up!" Margaret screamed.

"Don't just stand there," Regina commanded. "Come and help."

Their lifelong friend could only watch as the two sisters took out his car keys and wrapped up his body in a flowery bed sheet.

CHAPTER FIVE

"The girls suffered from what I call the 'Lord of the Flies' syndrome," Clark said. "Here they are hanging out with drug dealers, obtaining guns, killing men in the basement. There is no parental figure in sight! They are left to fend for themselves and the end result is murder and mayhem."

With the dead body in the basement, both sisters peeked out their window, waiting for dark.

Confident that the entire neighborhood was asleep, they opened the door and carried Oscar's body out of the home.

The three girls struggled carrying the dead weight, wrapping his body with a comforter and the flowered bed sheet.

They opened up the trunk and placed the body inside.

"What are you guys doing?" a woman yelled from a window across the street.

The girls looked up startled.

"We're getting rid of some furniture" Regina called out. "No worries."

The girls waved at the neighbor as she moved away from the window.

"Nosy bitch," Regina whispered.

Margaret giggled. Veronica still scared, said nothing.

They got into the vehicle and drove to a vacant lot where they took out Oscar's body again.

"This is hard work," Regina complained. "Shit!"

They plopped the body on the ground, looking at it for a beat before Regina reached back into the trunk. She pulled out a bottle of nail polish remover and poured the liquid over the tarp.

"Are you sure that's gonna work?" Margaret asked.

"It says 'highly flammable'," Regina said, shrugging her shoulders.

Margaret lit a match and set the material on fire.

The flame went up immediately, the girls could feel the warmth on their faces in the cold Chicago night.

"Told you this shit would work!" Regina said.

Then as fast as the flame started, it quickly died down.

"Light another one," Regina said.

Margaret threw down another match, getting the flames going again as Regina doused the tarp with the remaining nail polish remover.

Satisfied, the girls quickly got back into the Camaro and drove off.

**

An anonymous call came into police headquarters reporting the fire in the vacant lot. The caller investigated further, however, and saw Oscar's arm sticking out through the fire. He called 911 again with a sense of urgency, telling them of the body.

CHAPTER SIX

When police on scene identified Oscar Velazquez' partially burned body, their initial knee-jerk reaction was that this was the work of a local street gang, a drug deal gone awry. But when they found the nail polish remover bottle, however, they quickly realized that this was the work of amateurs. A jealous girlfriend maybe.

Meanwhile, the DeFrancisco sisters cruised around town over the following days, trying to pawn off the Camaro.

"This is where the sisters make the guys in 'Dumb and Dumber' look like geniuses," Clark said. "They had only pre-planned the front end of the murder. Like most impulsive killers, they had no idea what to do after. Their greed took over and they decide to sell the Camaro. They have no papers for it, duh, and really can only sell a stolen vehicle to a thug. They find no takers as even the dumbest street gang member isn't going to buy a hot car from two teenaged girls. So they cruise around town and Oscar's brother spots them in the car."

The girls, failing in their sales efforts, would later abandon he vehicle behind a storefront and set it on fire.

**

The day after Oscar's killing, a mutual friend named Jessica Benitez stopped by the house. Jessica went downstairs and watched Margaret mop up a stain of blood near the basement steps.

"The hell is that?" she asked.

Margaret said nothing as she poured bleach over the blood, scrubbing hard.

"Dude bled all over the floor," Regina said. "But only after Margaret kicked him in the head. We called him over, told this idiot we'd have a threesome with him. Then we robbed his ass."

"But the blood stain on the floor-" Jessica asked, watching Margaret clean up.

"We killed a guy," Margaret said without remorse.

"He was going to kill us!" Regina said. "Margaret shot him in the back of the head. We searched his body and found a gun in his waistband. Then we wrapped him up in plastic and put him in his car."

"Holy shit, girl," Jessica.

"We're about to go on the run," Margaret announced.

"Aren't you scared?" Jessica asked, looking back down at the blood stain in the basement.

"I ain't scared of nothing," Margaret said. "You should have seen his head when I shot him. His brain oozed out like cheese."

Margaret made a rolling motion with her hands.

Jessica then accompanied Margaret to the store she purchased a bottle of blonde hair dye for her "disguise."

"We see here how the whole street gang culture has influenced the behavior of these girls," Clark said. "At any point in time, Veronica or Jessica could have went straight to the police. But they get caught up in the drama of the moment. The so-called 'loyalty' to their friend who, quite frankly, would shoot them up in a heartbeat if they knew that they were going to be a snitch."

Going off the tip from Oscar's brother, the police show up to question both Regina and Margaret. The duo denied ever seeing Oscar.

They then go to interview Veronica Garcia.

They found the jittery fifteen year old to be a different story, however. The teen quickly crumbled under the pressure of questioning and told the police the entire story.

Feeling the heat, the DeFrancisco sisters go on the run...

CHAPTER SEVEN

For all of their stupidity in committing the murder, the DeFrancisco sisters deftly avoided capture for almost two years.

They decided to split up. Margaret would go to live with their maternal aunt in Roscoe, Illinois, an hour and a half drive away from where they lived. Roscoe was a small town with less then 10,000 people, a far cry from the drug infested streets of Chicago. Margaret's worst dreams were now realized. She was now a nerd who had to stay inside all day long, living in a boring cul-de-sac with no street gang action. Neighbors would remark that they would never see her and if hey did she would quickly go back inside.

Living underground without detection, it took a broadcast of the television show AMERICA'S MOST WANTED to generate an anonymous tip which led to Margaret's whereabouts. Police staked out her aunt's apartment and entered, finding Margaret in her bedroom with a blank look on her face.

"My feelings were hurt bad because she (my wife) did something behind my back," Margaret's uncle by marriage said later. "I knew (police) were going to find her anyway."

Seven months later, Regina was captured in Dallas living with her Latin King boyfriend, Johnny Rivera.

Initially, she did not even know where the gang banger lived. She just knew the town, Laredo, and she journeyed there by bus. Regina would eventually find him, locating one of his relatives. She would live under an alias and claimed that she worked as a maid.

Police knew better. Regina made money by selling drugs under the Latin King banner.

Unlike Margaret, Regina had evaded the scrutiny of the America's Most Wanted viewers.

Her capture came about because she could not stop hanging out with the wrong crowd.

Two sheriffs were had mistakenly arrived at her boyfriend's apartment, wanting to serve a warrant to someone else.

Rivera allowed the deputies to enter his apartment but he had left a marijuana flake on his table. Police searched the apartment further and found several packages of crack cocaine ready to be sold.

The deputies arrested Rivera. They searched inside the apartment and interviewed Regina, who was groggy from a cocaine high. She showed them her false Texas identification and they let her go.

But the deputies smelled something fishy on her aside from marijuana. They had the apartment manager set up a meeting with her. She arrived at the complex in an SUV with another man. The police approached and the SUV sped away.

The high-speed chase down residential Dallas streets reached upwards of 90 mph. The SUV then slammed into a center median, the front tires blowing out.

Regina got out of the car and tried to sprint away. A deputy tackled her and they fell to the ground, her cell phone skidding across the gravel road. Sifting through her pockets, the officer found over $1,500 cash.

She was taken to Dallas County Jail where they discovered her true identity.

"We pulled her out of jail," said a Deputy Dodson. "I asked to see one of her tattoos, and she showed me...I called her by name, but she never said a word to me. She knew it was over."

She was then extradited to Illinois to stand trial for the murder of Oscar Velazquez.

CHAPTER EIGHT

The trial of the two women began in July of 2004 and both sisters pleaded not guilty by reason of self-defense.

But their friend, Veronica Garcia, had cut a deal with prosecutors in return for a lesser sentence. She would provide the testimony that would damn the two sisters to prison.

Garcia said that she didn't know what the sisters had planned. She had simply provided the gun to the DeFrancisco's which she thought would be used for a robbery only.

"I didn't see her shoot Oscar," Veronica said.

The prosecution brought forth additional witnesses in Jessica Benitez, Luciana Macias, and Maria Constantino, the neighbor.

"Both of them told me that they killed Oscar," Jessica said. "Margaret kicked him in the head so he could die faster."

"I saw them load the body into the back of the Camaro," Constantino said. "Regina told me that she planned out the killing."

Margaret, however, maintained their innocence. She said that Oscar came to the apartment angry because the sisters had tricked him out of one-thousand dollars.

"I shot him to protect Regina," Margaret said.

"Then why didn't you tell the reporting officer what happened?" the prosecution attorney asked.

"We would've got in trouble," Margaret said. "If I told the truth, I would've been there longer."

Regina DeFrancisco would also take the stand and claim self-defense as well.

"I came out of my bedroom," Regina said. "And he was there, cursing and screaming. He pulled a gun on me. I thought I was going to die. I curled up on the floor, in a fetal position. I begged for my life. Then I heard a gunshot and saw Margaret standing over Oscar, holding a gun."

"Whose idea was it to dispose of the body?"

"Veronica knew of this vacant lot," Regina said. "It was her idea."

The jury would deliberate for over six and a half hours. Regina would be found guilty of murder. Margaret's jury, however, was unable to convict her. There was and 11 to 1 deadlock with one juror believing that she should be acquitted. The juror did not believe that someone so young could commit murder.

Margaret was then released from custody and told to await retrial. She had a baby during this time, a girl, and would find work as a nursing assistant while she awaited another trial.

Four months later, Margaret would be given another day in court. Veronica Garcia would once again be the star witness for the prosecution, detailing the exact same testimony as before.

There would be no deadlock in this second go around as Margaret would be convicted of first-degree murder.

Regina would be sentenced to 35 years in prison while Margaret would be sentenced to 46 years. Both women are now jailed at the Dwight Correctional Center. They have each filed appeals which have been denied.

"The girls cared nothing about Oscar Velazquez," Clark said. "In the end, they remained true to their own narcissistic nature. They only cared about what was happening to the next. They cared about nothing about the now fatherless children Oscar Velazquez would leave behind nor about the fact that the took his life."

Veronica Garcia was jailed for five years. She served her full sentence and has since been released.

"This is a cautionary tale if there ever was one," Clark said. "The sisters had it all. They had access to one of the finest schools in their state. Yet they chose to throw it all away for short money and the cheap thrill of the 'thug life.' In the end, they got to see what the 'thug life' was really all about. Mindless violence where everyone is out for themselves, especially when there is a plea bargain to be made. They could have had it all had they stayed on the straight and narrow. Now they have nothing."